Arsenal

Extraordinary images of an amazing club

Foreword by Arsène Wenger

hamlyn

PREVIOUS PAGES: The home changing room at Highbury with the Arsenal kits hanging on pegs ready for the match against Leeds United on 5 November 1938.

RIGHT: Fans arrive at Highbury for a match against Everton, 1 January 1972.

FOLLOWING PAGES: Thierry Henry celebrates his winning goal with Alexander Hleb in the first leg of the second round Champions League tie with Real Madrid at the Bernabeu, 21 February 2006.

An Hachette Livre UK Company

First published in Great Britain in 2007 by
Hamlyn, a division of Octopus Publishing Group Ltd
2–4 Heron Quays, London E14 4JP
www.octopusbooks.co.uk

Copyright © Octopus Publishing Group Ltd 2007

ISBN-13: 978-0-600-61705-1
ISBN-10: 0-600-61705-X

A CIP catalogue record for this book is available from
the British Library

Printed and bound in Slovenia
Colour reproduction by Dot Gradations Ltd, UK

10 9 8 7 6 5 4 3 2 1

CONTENTS

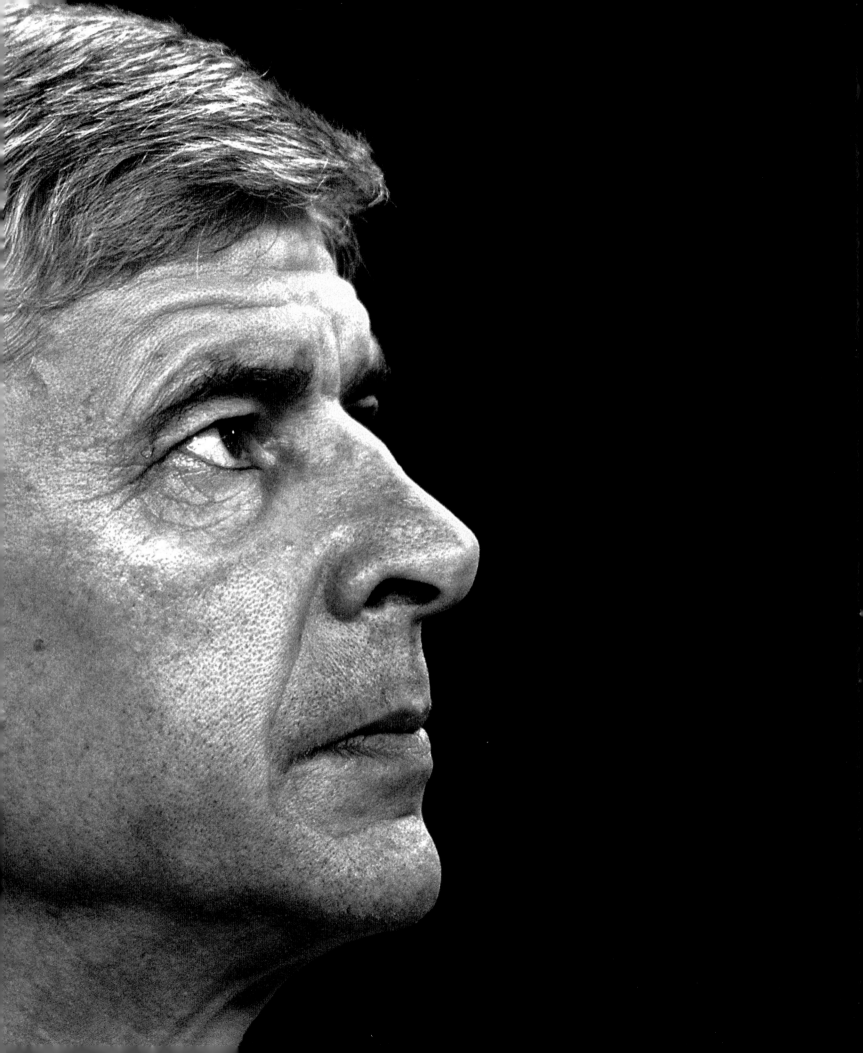

ABOVE: Three survivors from the Royal Arsenal days, John McBean, Gavin Crawford and Bill Julian, the Club's first professional captain, watch Arsenal lose 2-0 to Chelsea at Highbury, 20 March 1948.

LEFT: Goalkeeper Harold Crawford makes a save against Manchester City at the Manor Ground, 2 November 1912. City won 4-0.

FOLLOWING PAGES: Woolwich Arsenal fans enjoy a 2-0 win against Newcastle at the Manor Ground, 22 September 1906. The Club, playing under the guises of Dial Square, Royal Arsenal and Woolwich Arsenal, survived due to the several thousand Woolwich factory workers, munitions makers, soldiers and dockers who embodied the Club's industrial origins and made south London such an uncomfortable place for visiting teams. The Newcastle Echo called it United's 'annual trip to hell' and one visiting player said 'a journey to the molten interior of the Earth's core would be more pleasant and comfortable'.

...ection of the Crowd on Spion Kop

RY'S MACA

Manor Ground 22·9·06.

ABOVE: Commissionaire on duty in the Marble Halls, 1953.

RIGHT: The magnificent East Stand art deco façade at Highbury, May 2006.

ABOVE: Without Henry Norris's political and personal influence, ambition, determination and, some would say, callous disregard for the Club's roots and supporters, Arsenal might have vanished. Instead, taking over as chairman in 1910, he manoeuvred a club with only £19 in its accounts towards both the latent reservoir of support in Islington and top-flight football. His greatest achievement was, perhaps, his appointment of Herbert Chapman as manager in 1925.

RIGHT: Building work on the North Terrace at Highbury continues, 25 August 1913. Chairman Henry Norris wanted a location for his new club with a large local population and good transport links. He settled on the site at Highbury which had three Tube stations nearby. When news of Norris's plans began circulating Tottenham and Clapton Orient objected, begging their fans not to go and support their new rivals, while local residents began to protest. Norris used his newspaper contacts to starve protest action groups of the oxygen of publicity, while convincing local businesses they would profit from the thousands of new customers passing their shop windows.

23

ABOVE: An early shot of Highbury, taken during the 2-0 win against Fulham on 14 March 1914, shows architect Archibald Leitch's trademark multi-span stand roof. Huge canopies at the back of the stand protected fans from rain while construction was finalised. Leitch became known as football's first engineer due to his work at stadiums such as Ibrox, Stamford Bridge, Goodison Park, Old Trafford and White Hart Lane. A 2-1 victory over Leicester Fosse six months earlier marked the Club's first game at Highbury. George Jobey, scorer of Arsenal's first goal, was injured in the game and taken home on the back of a milkman's cart!

ABOVE: Apart from cosmetic changes, Highbury remained unchanged from the mid-1950s until the early 1990s, when the Taylor Report following the Hillsborough disaster in 1989 advised that grounds become all-seater. In 1993 the redeveloped North Bank proved to be the perfect modern architectural accompaniment to the East and West Stands. The Club installed a mural while the construction took place. This picture shows a match between Arsenal and Sheffield Wednesday on 29 August 1992. Arsenal won 2-1.

RIGHT: Workmen attending to the scoreboard at the Clock End, 28 August 1930. Chapman advocated a 45-minute clock to add to the enjoyment of the fans. This iconic symbol of the Club was quickly altered to a normal clock on the insistence of the FA which felt it might undermine the referee's authority. Initially housed in the Laundry End, it was moved to its spiritual home when the former was roofed. It now stands proudly at Emirates Stadium.

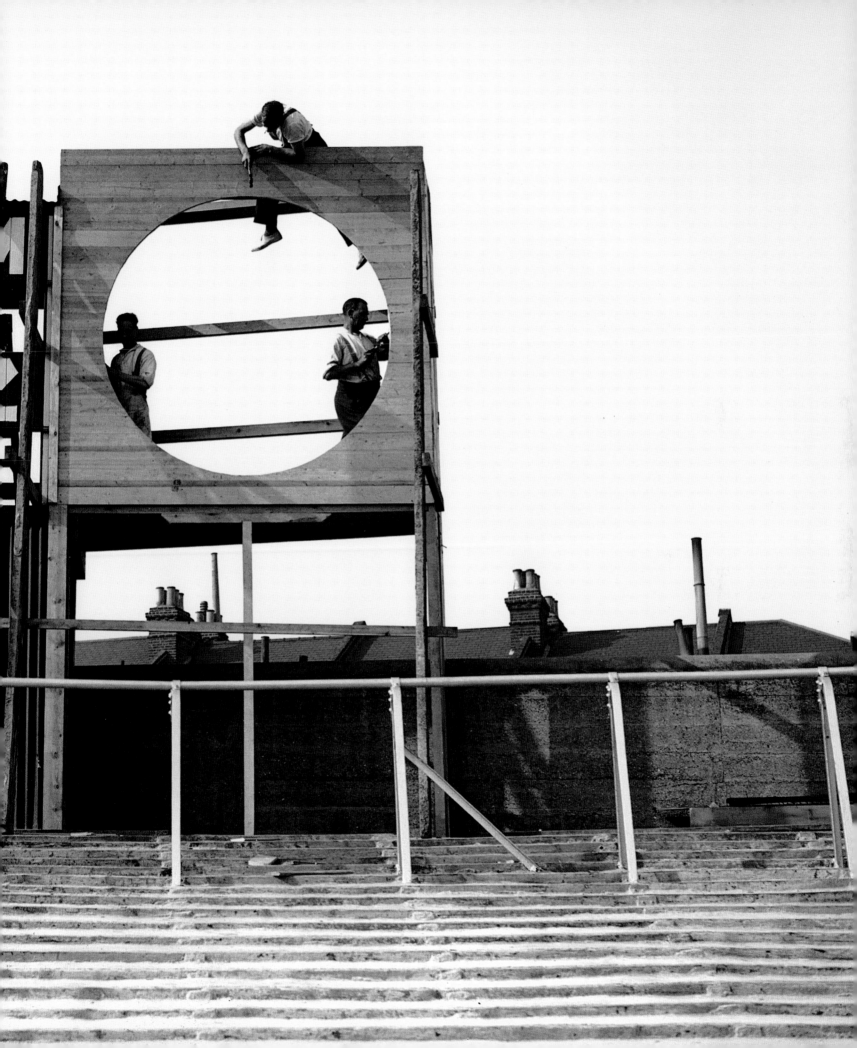

ABOVE: Demolition work on the old East Stand takes place, 21 April 1936. The new incarnation would include a boardroom, tearooms, the Horseshoe Bar - one of the largest in the world - mahogany-panelled offices, marble halls, heated floors in the changing rooms, a public address system, a state-of-the-art indoor gym and treatment room plus a dedicated broadcast booth for the BBC, the first of its kind.

RIGHT: A construction worker teeters above the East Stand construction, 17 June 1936. The famous art deco East Stand cost £130,000 and opened in October 1936.

ABOVE: The pitch is marked out at Emirates Stadium for the very first time, 18 July 2006.

LEFT: Commissionaires clear the pitch after a match, late 1940s.

ABOVE: In August 1936, Arsenal players including Alex White took part in a practice match at Highbury. The East Stand is shown in the background with extensive scaffolding.

RIGHT: Workmen watch a trial match at Highbury from the scaffolding of the East Stand on 15 August 1936.

ABOVE: Gilberto scores the equalizer against Aston Villa on 19 August 2006 during the first competitive match at the Emirates Stadium. This goal made him the first Arsenal player to score at the ground. The final score, Arsenal 1 Aston Villa 1.

LEFT: Thierry Henry pays his respects to Highbury as he celebrates his third goal in the 4-2 win over Wigan Athletic, the Club's final match at their home of 93 years, 7 May 2006. The man who ended up scoring more goals than anyone else at Highbury - 137, and he assisted in just as many - is probably the finest embodiment of it with his unforced style and classic elegance.

ABOVE: The Prince of Wales, later Edward VIII, is introduced to the team by Alex James before the match against Chelsea which marked the opening of the West Stand at Highbury, 10 December 1932. Costing £50,000, it was a testament to the vision and pioneering spirit of the Club, and offered fans protection from the weather, luxurious padded seats and an executive suite with private entrance, electric passenger lift and heated lounges. Arsenal celebrated in style with a 4–1 victory.

RIGHT: The new West Stand under construction at Highbury, 18 July 1932. The Islington Gazette said the completed stand was a tribute to the 'football brains and showmanship' of Herbert Chapman. Stadium development on a scale never previously seen enabled Arsenal to generate increased revenues which they could reinvest, often spectacularly, in the transfer market. This earned them the nickname The Bank Of England Club.

FOLLOWING PAGES: Emirates Stadium opens for the very first time for Dennis Bergkamp's testimonial, Arsenal v Ajax, 22 July 2006. Arsenal won 2–1. It was with the same pioneering spirit of the men who developed Highbury that the Club, nearly a century on, took the short but bold journey to Emirates Stadium, a modern home steeped in the values and spirit of the Club where Arsenal can continue to progress.

ABOVE: Arsenal players take a break during the filming of *The Arsenal Stadium Mystery*, 1 July 1939. Alf Fields recalled visiting Ealing Studios for the shoot. He said: 'They were filming *The Thief Of Baghdad* on one side of us, and a war film on the other, so the place was full of harem girls and soldiers!'

ABOVE: A scene from the film, *The Arsenal Stadium Mystery*. In 1952 a Spanish newspaper headline screamed: 'Arsenal Player Murdered During A Match. Scotland Yard Investigates!' The article continued: 'The players who took part in the match have been questioned, as well as the referee, who would appear to be the murderer'. The editorial office had mistaken film publicity for fact.

RIGHT: The Arsenal squad line up with their trophy haul in 1931. The trophies are, from left to right, the Northampton Hospital Shield, the 'Evening News' Cricket Cup, the League Championship Trophy, the Sheriff of London's Shield, the Charity Shield and the Combination Cup.

ABOVE: A large crowd enjoys a pre-season trial game between Arsenal's first and second teams at Highbury, 15 August 1925. Harry Woods (left) played in the first team and Hugh Lafferty (right) was in the second team. Arsenal still hold open training sessions at Emirates Stadium that Club members can attend.

ABOVE: The squad take a brisk walk up Avenell Road on their first day of pre-season training, 6 August 1935.

ABOVE: The victorious 1936 FA Cup winning squad. Back row from left, George Male, Jack Crayston, Alex Wilson, Herbie Roberts, Ted Drake, Eddie Hapgood. Middle row, George Allison, Joe Hulme, Ray Bowden, Alex James, Cliff Bastin, Tom Whittaker. Front row, Bob John and Wilf Copping.

RIGHT: England played world champions Italy on 14 November 1934 in a fixture which was to be known as the 'Battle of Highbury'. England won 3–2 in a fiercely contested match that left three players with broken bones. The England team featured seven Arsenal players: Wilf Copping, Ray Bowden, George Male, Frank Moss, Ted Drake, Eddie Hapgood and Cliff Bastin.

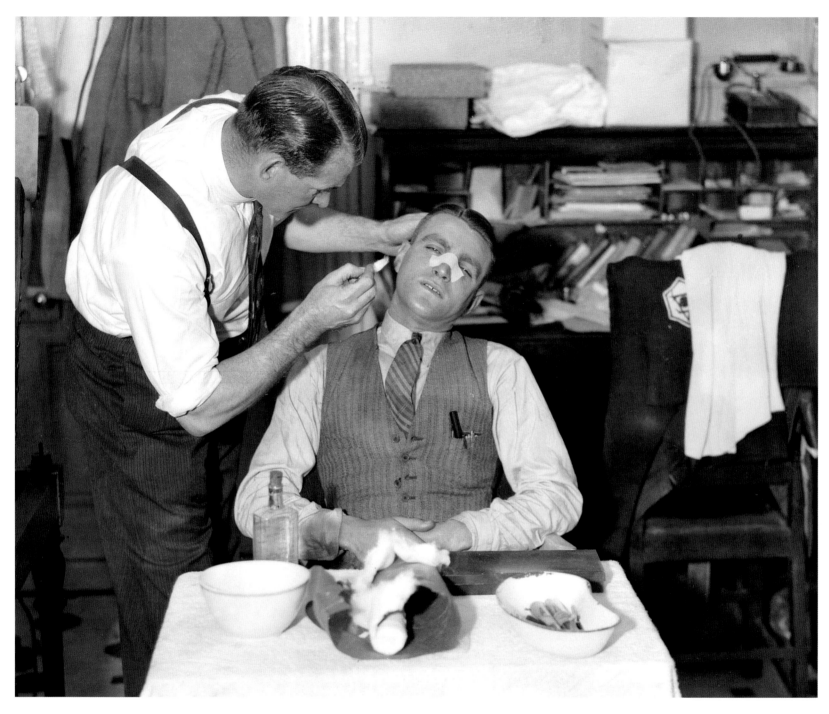

ABOVE: Eddie Hapgood receives treatment for a broken nose the day after the Battle of Highbury, 14 November 1934.

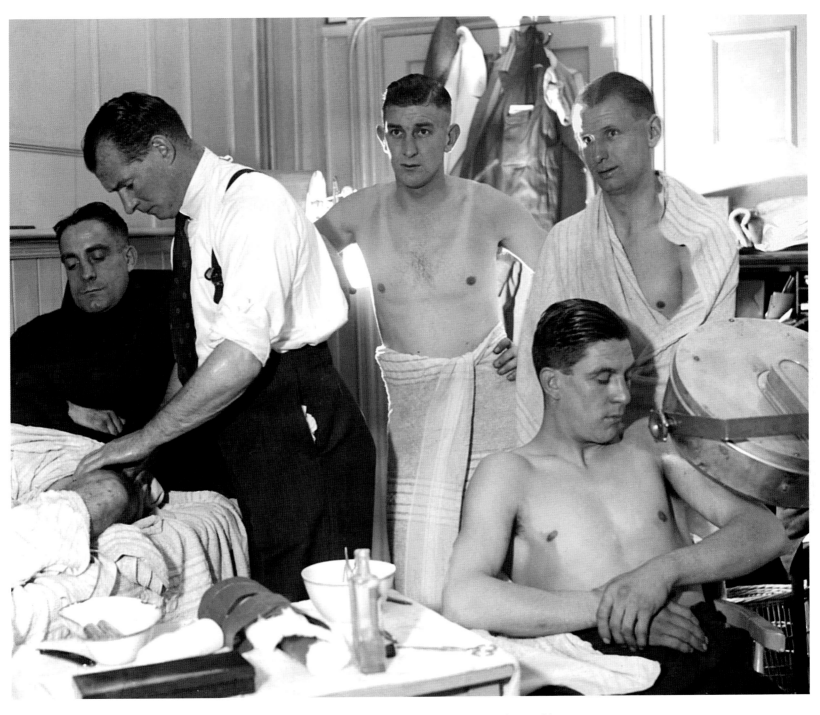

ABOVE: Tom Whittaker examines Wilf Copping in the Highbury treatment room as Frank Moss, Cliff Bastin and Ted Drake wait their turn after the bruising encounter with Italy. Whittaker was the England trainer and he had a busy night.

RIGHT: Tom Parker forces
his way through the crowd
on his way to the dressing room
for the Club's first League
Championship presentation,
2 May 1931.

ABOVE: Arriving in tin hats for ARP training at Highbury are, from left, Cliff Bastin, Tom Whittaker, George Male and George Marks, 13 October 1939. During the Second World War, Highbury was used as an Air Raid Precaution Unit. The dressing rooms were used to nurse casualties and local families sheltered in the stadium. The North Bank roof was destroyed in 1945 and it was not until 1954 that the Club was able to countenance the rebuilding of it, financed by a grant from the War Damages Commission.

LEFT: Arsenal's Sergeant Wilf Copping and Gunner Denis Compton arrive to play for the Army against the Football Association at Selhurst Park for a wartime exhibition game designed to improve national morale, 20 January 1940.

RIGHT: In August 1945 members of the Arsenal team, along with manager Squadron Leader T. J. Whittaker, travelled for a weekend tour of Germany. The team played against service teams for the entertainment of the troops.

ABOVE: Christopher Wreh celebrates Arsenal's fifth goal in a 5-0 win against Wimbledon at Highbury, 18 April 1998.

RIGHT: Ian Wright is overjoyed after scoring his 100th goal for Arsenal. Unashamedly theatrical and with an ego as wide as his smile, he was a swaggeringly exuberant executioner and entertainer. The record books show a staggering strike ratio, but it is the sensational manner of so many of his strikes and extravagant celebrations which stay fresh in the memory.

ABOVE: Bob McNab signs George Armstrong's plaster cast at Highbury, 17 August 1973. 'Geordie' Armstrong was a workaholic winger of perpetual motion whose capacity for tracking back frustrated countless opposition raids and made him a firm crowd favourite.

LEFT: Ted Drake is finally carried off the field unconscious during a match at Brentford, 18 April 1938. He had played on after breaking his wrist and receiving nine stitches for a gash to his head. Arsenal lost 3-0.

ABOVE: Bob Wilson celebrates the third and decisive goal in the 3-0 Intercity Fairs Cup Final second leg victory over Anderlecht, 28 April 1970. Victory ended 17 trophy-less years on an electric night at Highbury. A combination of courage, intelligence and sheer hard graft transformed Wilson from an unpaid amateur who made his debut in 1963 into a cornerstone of the Club's re-emergence.

ABOVE: Bob Wilson celebrates Ray Kennedy's goal in the 1-0 win at White Hart Lane which secured the League Championship, 4 May 1971. The FA Cup would follow days later.

ABOVE: Manchester United goalkeeper Fabien Barthez shows his anguish after his mistake enables Thierry Henry to complete a 3-1 victory at Highbury, 25 November 2001.

LEFT: Thierry Henry scores the aforementioned goal (see above). Patrick Vieira said: 'What he has achieved has largely been the result of sheer hard work and dedication, allied to passion and natural talent.'

ABOVE: Arsenal captain Frank McLintock collides with the referee during the final League game of the 1970–71 season on 3 May 1971. Arsenal won the match 1-0 to clinch the League title.

RIGHT: George Graham is booked by Clive Thomas during Arsenal's 2-1 win over Wolverhampton Wanderers at Highbury, 8 April 1972. Graham went on to become one of Arsenal's most successful post-war managers. It was Graham's attention to detail and readiness to adapt to circumstances which fostered a spirit in his sides that produced unexpected results and ended a prolonged spell without trophies.

ABOVE: Les Compton leaps for the ball against Chelsea, 23 April 1949. Arsenal lost 2-1.

LEFT: Arsenal goalkeeper George Swindin kicks the ball upfield during a match against Chelsea at Stamford Bridge on the 9 October 1937. The game ended in a 2-2 draw.

ABOVE: Arsenal right back Tom Parks beats a Newcastle United player to the ball during a 2-2 draw at Highbury, 2 October 1926.

RIGHT: Action from one of the most memorable games at Highbury – Arsenal against Manchester United on 1 February 1958, which United won 5-4. It was United's last match before the fatal Munich air disaster. Arsenal players are (left to right) Jack Kelsey, Jim Fotheringham and Dennis Evans.

ABOVE: Alan Ball, George Armstrong and George Graham prepare to face a Derby County free-kick, 12th February 1972. Arsenal won 2-0.

ABOVE: The East Stand at Highbury contained a gentlemen's dining salon complete with the only cocktail bar fitted inside a football ground, pictured here in November 1938. It's a testament to the architects that both of Highbury's Art Deco stands remained largely unchanged for the next 70 years and earned heritage protection. The East Stand façade still has Grade II listed status and remains a central feature of the Highbury Square residential development.

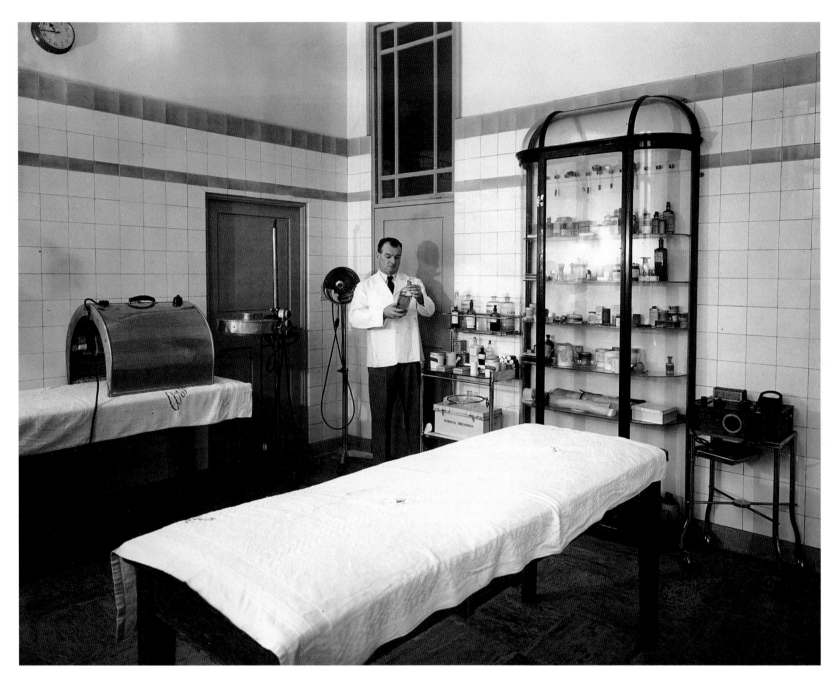

ABOVE: Tom Whittaker in the new medical room at Highbury, November 1938. Whittaker played for Arsenal for six years, retiring after suffering a broken knee cap. Wishing to stay within the game, he joined the coaching staff at the Club and studied as a physiotherapist. Having worked under Herbert Chapman and George Allison, he became Arsenal manager in 1947.

ABOVE: The home side changing room at Highbury with the Arsenal kits hanging on pegs, ready for the match against Leeds United on 5 November 1938.

LEFT: The interior of the bath and shower room at Highbury, 7 November 1936. Heated marble floors in the new East Stand changing rooms were a welcome additional feature for the players who both trained and played at the stadium.

ABOVE: A cleaner scrubs the Arsenal crest in the entrance to the Marble Halls, Highbury, 1951.

ABOVE: Arsenal groundsmen Fred Virgo and Jimmy Mosie get ready for the new season as the goal posts are erected in front of the North Bank in August 1977.

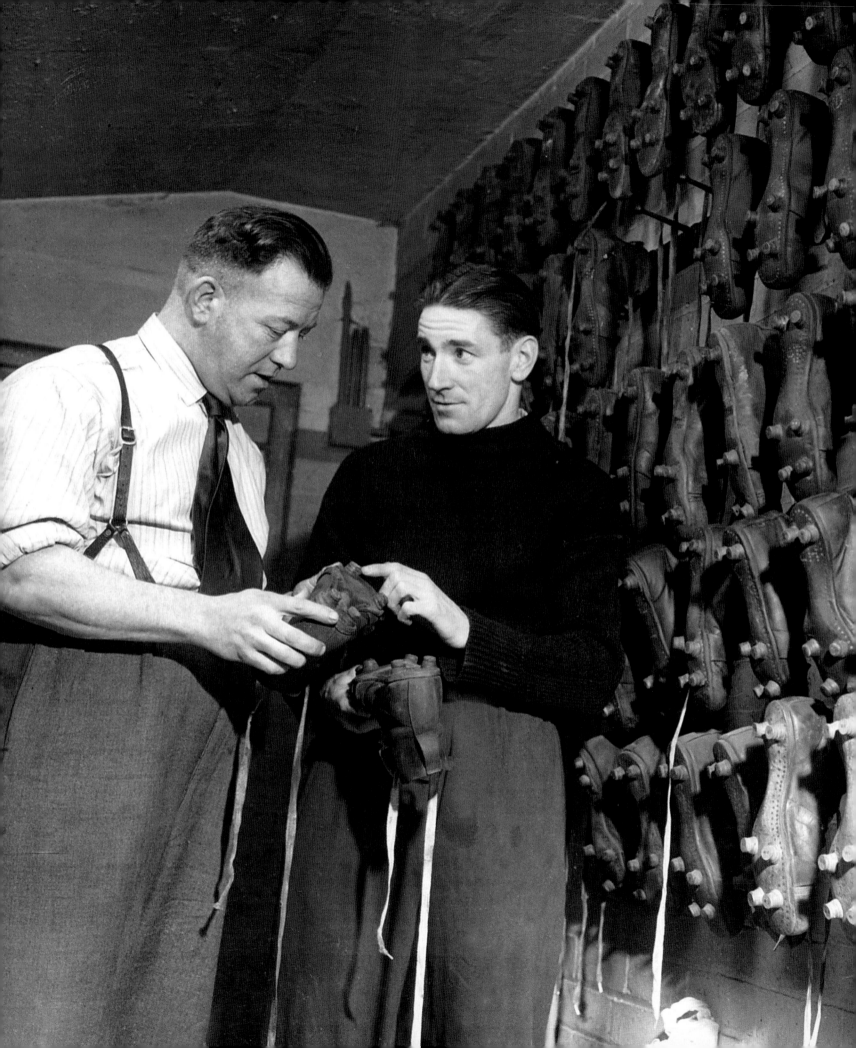

ABOVE: Laundry is completed, 30 January 1950. The hooped socks, like the white sleeves, were introduced by Herbert Chapman to enable the players to quickly identify each other on the pitch without looking up too high. These were blue and white. In the 1970s technological advances meant that the red dye on the preferred red and white hooped socks no longer ran to create pink garments!

LEFT: Jimmy Logie discusses repairing his boots with handyman Dan Cripps, 30 January 1950. Logie signed in June 1939 but within weeks he had joined the Navy and spent the Second World War serving on trawlers. It wasn't until after the war that the quick inside right was able to demonstrate his exceptional close control and shrewdly timed passing.

ABOVE: Artist Yates Wilson painted the Arsenal squad for the cover of the then-popular John Bull magazine. The painting was titled Tom Whittaker's Secret, and featured in the magazine on 6 December 1947. Here the manager, centre, receives the painting from the editor, left, and the artist.

RIGHT: The players recreate the Yates Wilson painting (above) which was reproduced in John Bull magazine, 6 December 1947. From left, Ronnie Rooke, Leslie Compton, Archie Macaulay, James Logie, Wally Barnes, Reg Lewis, Paddy Sloan, George Male, Bryn Jones and Denis Compton.

ABOVE: The Arsenal office staff sort through the post from supporters requesting tickets for the 1936 FA Cup Final against Sheffield United.

ABOVE: The Arsenal team take a look at a camera at Highbury after playing in the first football match to be filmed live on television. Arsenal's first team took on the reserves in September 1937. Ten years earlier the first live radio broadcast of a football match had been at Highbury.

ABOVE: Arsenal and Fulham players take part in an instructional film for the Football Association at Hendon in September 1947.

ABOVE: The Arsenal manager and players look on as under-soil heating cables are laid under the Highbury pitch, 24 April 1964. From left, Billy Wright, George Eastham, Billy McCullough, Alan Skirton, Ian Ure, Johnny McLeod and Jim Magill. Ever since, Arsenal have invested in new technologies to maintain their famed, immaculate playing surface. One of the most important criteria for the Club during the move to Emirates Stadium, was to keep the standard of the pitch as high as possible.

ABOVE: Denis Compton and Middlesex captain W. J. Edrich call the toss before the benefit cricket match for Compton on the Highbury pitch.

LEFT AND ABOVE: Some club flirtations with new technologies were less successful than others. In this training session each player wore a hearing device while coach Ron Greenwood issued instructions to them via a microphone, 5 August 1960. Reception was only one-way – the players could not answer back!

ABOVE: A packed Highbury basks under floodlights as Arsenal take on Rangers, 17 October 1951. This was the second game under floodlights at Highbury and Arsenal won 3-2. The first official match was against Hapoel Tel Aviv one month earlier on 19 September, which Arsenal won 6-1.

ABOVE: Charles Buchan watches goalkeeper Dan Lewis practise his kicking during preparations for the 1927 FA Cup Final. Arsenal were to narrowly lose the final to Cardiff City, a speculative shot slipping under Lewis' body and into the net. Lewis blamed the starch on his new shirt for the error. Subsequently, for half a century, goalkeepers' new shirts were washed by the Arsenal kit-man before being worn in a competitive match.

LEFT: Arthur Milton using the shooting gallery at Highbury, 1 December 1951. Milton was one of the many Arsenal players who played county cricket during the summer. He represented Gloucestershire.

ABOVE: Arsenal striker David Herd practises his heading technique at the Club's training ground on 22 July 1960.

RIGHT: Former Arsenal goalkeeper Alex Wilson demonstrates his own invention – a machine that projects footballs into the goalmouth – at Highbury in January 1950 as Leslie Compton and Jimmy Logie practise their aerial control against goalkeeper Ted Platt.

ABOVE: Muhammad Ali on his way to defeating British heavyweight champion Henry Cooper in the sixth round at Highbury, 21 May 1966.

LEFT: With the Highbury pitch covered by a protective surface prior to the World Heavyweight Championship title fight, an impromptu training session takes place, 17 May 1966. Highbury hosted many non-football events including cricket, hockey and rugby matches.

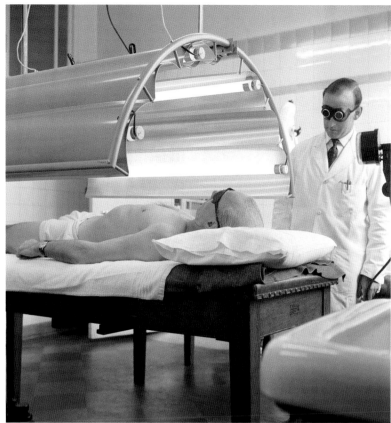

ABOVE: Arsenal physiotherapist Bertie Mee uses revolutionary new heat technology to treat an injured player in April 1961.

LEFT: Left to right, Bob John, Joe Hulme and Alex James trial 'sunlight' therapy treatment, 16 January 1931. The device was used to aid players' recovery from injury.

ABOVE: Coach Ernie Collet uses a new board to explain tactics in the dressing room, 20 March 1967.

RIGHT: George Allison talks tactics with the team, 1 November 1938. Allison revived the Club after the death of Herbert Chapman. He was allegedly told by Chapman shortly before he died, 'The team's played out, Mr Allison. We must rebuild'. Like his predecessor, Allison was shrewd in the transfer market, and signed talented players who brought a new desire to the side.

RIGHT: Tom Parker takes a swing as David Jack, Alex James and Herbert Chapman (from left to right) look on, 14 November 1929. Chapman was a firm advocate of mind over matter and felt golf would help his players relax, and also foster a sense of unity.

ABOVE: Bryn Jones and goalkeeper Ted Platt are cooled down by the groundsman while training on 1 August 1947.

ABOVE: England World Cup winner, Alan Ball, sprints around Highbury during a training session, 24 December 1971, just after joining the Gunners from Everton.

ABOVE: Jock Rutherford, a winger who played 222 League games for Arsenal from 1913–1926, in training on 30 October 1913. His son, John, also played in the 1925-26 season. John made only one first team appearance.

RIGHT: Training at Highbury, from left, Archie Clark, Reg Tricker, Dan Lewis, William Seddon and Bob John, 3 August 1927.

ABOVE: Wilson oversaw a series of psychology exercises in August 1936.

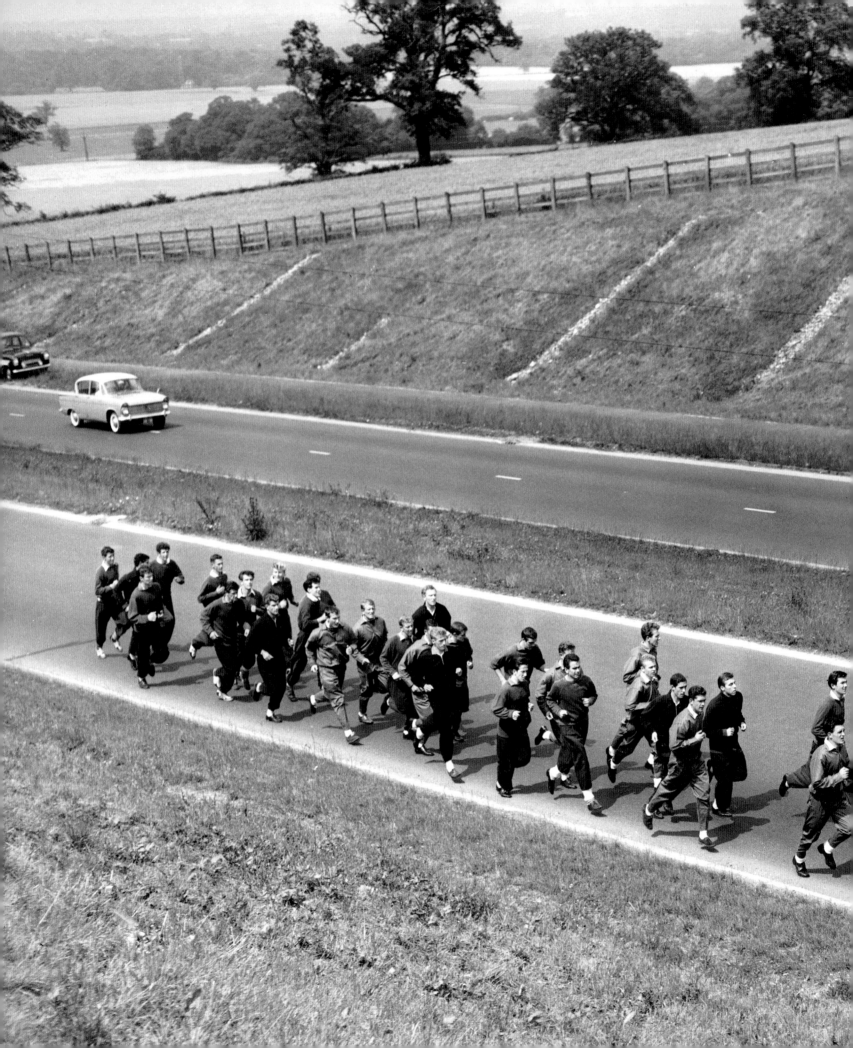

LEFT: The squad take a pre-season jog along the
A6 dual carriageway, July 1962.

RIGHT: Coach Dave Sexton, right, instructs
players at Highbury, from left, Frank McLintock,
Terry Neill, Peter Storey and Jon Sammels,
11 August 1967.

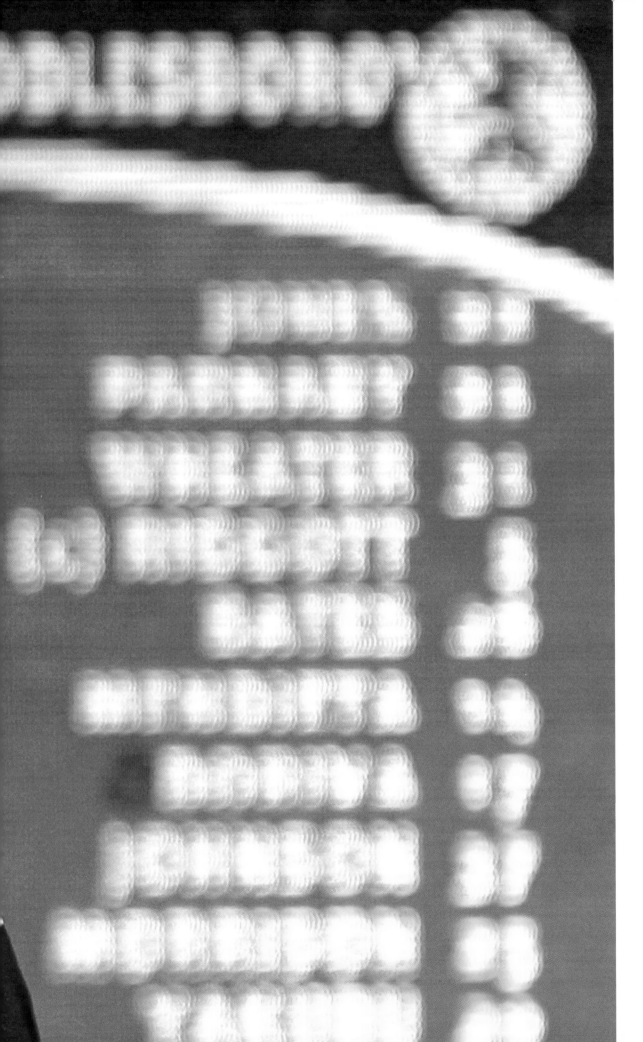

LEFT: Thierry Henry during a Club-record 7-0 Premiership win over Middlesbrough, 14 January 2006. The redcurrant commemorative kit was worn at Highbury throughout the stadium's final season and reflected the colour of the kit worn 93 years earlier during Highbury's inaugural season.

RIGHT: John Hollins and David O'Leary relax with the FA Cup during a break in pre-season training, 17 July 1979. O'Leary went on to make more Arsenal appearances - 722 in total - than any other player.

ABOVE: John Radford scores in a 3-1 win at Blackpool, 7 November 1970. Fit and fast, big and strong but with tactical intelligence, Radford's play made it possible for others to shine. His priceless asset was an ability to time his off-the-ball runs to maximum advantage.

ABOVE: Liam Brady celebrates a cool finish in a 1-0 win against Sheffield United at Highbury, 31 January 1976. 'Chippy' Brady had skill and a total vision of the pitch which often crossed that subtle boundary between sport and art. Moving smoothly and elegantly, always in total command of the ball, the slightly-built Dubliner's minimal backlift disguised his intentions until the last moment.

ABOVE: Dennis Bergkamp celebrates a goal in Arsenal's 2-2 League Cup semi-final first leg draw against Aston Villa at Highbury, 14 February 1996.

RIGHT: Charlie George, 1970. 'You might not always have agreed with what Charlie said or even the way he said it but you knew that when he talked about the Arsenal it came straight from his heart,' said Frank McLintock.

LEFT: Charlie George attends a pre-season photocall, 11 August 1972. Having not signed a new contract he had no number on his shirt.

ABOVE: Arsenal's new signings from Leyton Orient, Vic Groves (jumping) and Stan Charlton, enjoying their first day of training at Highbury, November 1955.

LEFT: Denis Compton, right, with brother Leslie at Highbury, 22 October 1947. Both Denis and Leslie played cricket for England as well as forging successful football careers. They enjoyed the distinction of being the only sportsmen who were members of a County Championship-winning side and an FA Cup-winning team in the same calendar year. In many ways, it can be claimed Denis Compton was the first media icon in British sport with his endorsement of Brylcreem and his subsequent nickname 'the Brylcreem boy'.

ABOVE: Arsenal captain Eddie Hapgood in August 1934 with his son, the Arsenal mascot.

RIGHT: Charlie Buchan leads out Jimmy Brain, Bill Harper and Alex Mackie, 1920s.

ABOVE: The fabled Arsenal back four, including captain Tony Adams, Steve Bould, Lee Dixon and Nigel Winterburn, raise their arms for offside against Panathiankos in the Makita International tournament on 3 August 1991. With David Seaman, and often supported by the coldly forbidding Martin Keown, they exuded telepathic understanding, authority, resilience and courage.

ABOVE: Ashley Cole, Patrick Vieira and Sol Campbell celebrate winning the League Championship, the second part of another Double, following a 1–0 win at Old Trafford, 8 May 2002.

ABOVE: Frank Stapleton receives treatment in the changing rooms, 2 April 1979. Strongly built, adroit, quick-minded and a selfless runner, Stapleton flowered as a performer of genuine stature when introduced to the side with Malcolm Macdonald. It was his aerial ability, unmatched by his peers in both timing and power, which is fondly remembered by many.

ABOVE: Frank McLintock and Jackie Collins in February 1979. Frank McLintock was the technical advisor on Jackie Collins' football movie *Yesterday's Hero*, which was released in November 1979.

ABOVE: Fans salute David Rocastle at the final match at Highbury. The morning that the announcement of David Rocastle's death was made was on the day that Arsenal hosted Tottenham in a Premiership clash, 31 March 2001. After a minute's silence, Arsenal went on to win 2-0 with, fittingly, Robert Pires wearing Rocastle's number 7 shirt scoring a goal reminiscent of the player known by fans as 'Rocky'.

RIGHT: Arsenal captain Patrick Vieira celebrates scoring his goal against rivals Tottenham at White Hart Lane while a Spurs fan throws a soft drink in his direction. Although the game ended in a 2-2 draw, the point was enough to secure the 2003-04 League title.

LEFT: Sol Campbell heads Arsenal into the lead during the Champions League Final against Barcelona, 17 May 2006. On the foundations of an inexperienced but impenetrable defence that tallied a record ten clean sheets, and a five-man midfield which supported Thierry Henry with flair and verve, the Gunners had defeated previous European champions Ajax, Real Madrid and Juventus among others on the way to the final. On a stormy night in Paris defiant Arsenal, down to 10-men for most of the game, fought valiantly and led for most of the evening, falling heroically short only at the very end of a journey which had captivated millions. Arsenal lost 2-1.

ABOVE: Pat Jennings prepares for the penalty shoot-out which decided the 1980 European Cup-Winners' Cup Final in Valencia's favour after a 0-0 draw. Calm, almost stately, Jennings infused his defenders with supreme confidence. Crowds were enraptured as hands like shovels plucked swirling crosses from the sky. Such was his longevity he had a testimonial for both north London clubs.

RIGHT: In the first European final to go to penalties, and the Club's 70th game of the season, Terry Neill and Don Howe cannot bear to watch the shoot-out against Valencia in Brussels, 14 May 1980 (see above). Arsenal lost 4-5 on penalties.

ABOVE: Arsenal applaud Dynamo Moscow off the pitch after a 5-0 defeat in a friendly match, October 1954. A year after the death of Stalin, Arsenal had been one of the first English teams to venture into Soviet Russia. It was not the first meeting between the clubs. In the immediate aftermath of the Second World War, a touring Dynamo, then arguably Europe's finest side, insisted that they met the famous Arsenal, who featured Stanley Matthews and Stan Mortenson as guest players in a game played at White Hart Lane.

LEFT: The Arsenal team at Croydon Airport en route to play Racing Club of Paris, 11 November 1930. The game was the first of 27 eagerly anticipated meetings with the prestigious French club in aid of Great War veterans. The matches made Arsenal and their players household names throughout western Europe. The French gave nicknames to many Arsenal stars including Le Feu d'Artfice (The Firework) for Cliff Bastin and Le Miracle (The Miracle) for Alex James.

ABOVE: Terry Neill, centre, with his assistant Wilf Dixon, left, and physio Fred Street, during a 3-2 defeat v West Ham at Highbury, 19 February 1977. Neill returned to Arsenal in 1976 to replace Bertie Mee, becoming the youngest manager in the history of the Club. He successfully steered Arsenal to three FA Cup Finals, winning the trophy in 1979 against Manchester United.

ABOVE: From left, manager Tom Whittaker, trainer Billy Milne and general assistant Danny Cripps during a 0-0 home draw with Portsmouth, 4 October 1947. After the Second World War, Arsenal were a very different club. Heavily in debt and with a damaged stadium, they were reliant on veteran players who had lost their best years. Nevertheless these men could be counted on and in 1947-48, Whittaker's first season as manager, the Club won the League title.

ABOVE: Arsène Wenger parades the FA Cup and Championship trophy, 17 May 1998. Wenger arrived with British tabloid headlines asking 'Arsène Who?' By the end of his first full season he had won the Double.

LEFT: Coach Don Howe gives his manager, Terry Neill, a lift during training at Highbury, 1978.

ABOVE: George Graham, a key player in the 1971 Double team, took charge of Arsenal in 1986. As a player he had been nicknamed the 'Stroller' for his style of play; as a manger he became famous for his fierce determination. Graham built his team on a resolute and hard-working back four and steered the team to the League Cup in 1987, Championships in 1989 and 1991, the domestic Cup 'Double' in 1993 and the European Cup Winners Cup in 1994.

RIGHT: Arsenal manager George Allison talks to journalists prior to the 1936 FA Cup Final against Sheffield United. A former journalist himself, who had often taken the arduous journey from Fleet Street to report on Woolwich Arsenal, Allison was a master of publicity. Upon taking over as manager, he cemented Arsenal's status by making sure that the Club regularly appeared in newsreels.

RIGHT: Tom Whittaker pictured in front of the trophy cabinet in his office in 1953. Whittaker once said: 'Someone has to drive himself too hard for Arsenal. Herbert Chapman worked himself to death for the Club and if it is my fate, I am happy to accept it'. It was tragically prophetic that having served the Club as player, trainer and manager Whittaker died in 1956 while hiding his health problems from his employers, as he laboured to keep Arsenal at the top of the game. It is the ultimate tribute that for much of his working life he managed to do this.

RIGHT: A huge crowd arrives at Highbury for the north London derby, 31 January 1934. Crowds in excess of 70,000 were common in the 1930s as Arsenal, using Chapman's famous WM system to mix tight collective defence with devastating counter-attack, became champions in 1931, 1933, 1934, 1935 and 1938.

ABOVE: A referee warns spectators that the match will be abandoned if there are any more fireworks as Arsenal play Manchester City at Highbury on 2 November 1957.

ABOVE: Police try to eject supporters as they invade the pitch prior to the match against Manchester United on 26 August 1973. The game ended in a goalless draw.

ABOVE: Arsenal supporters gather at Waterloo station before making their way to Fratton Park to see Arsenal play Portsmouth in the FA Cup on 13 February 1932.

RIGHT: Arsenal fans at Kings Cross to catch the special trains to Huddersfield for an FA Cup semi-final against Grimsby Town, 21 March 1936. Arsenal won 1–0 and Cliff Bastin scored the winning goal.

LEFT: Young fans cheer on Arsenal during a friendly with Glasgow Rangers in one of the first floodlit games at Highbury, 1 December 1951. Herbert Chapman had promoted the use of floodlights to offset competition from speedway and dog racing. Floodlights were installed at Highbury in 1931 but the game's rulers did not sanction their use until the 1950s. The first floodlit game at Highbury was a Boxers v Jockeys charity match in April 1951.

ABOVE: Local newsagents pose with newspapers anticipating an amazing Double. This picture was taken on 7 May 1971, the day before the Club took on Liverpool in the FA Cup Final and four days after they secured the Championship.

LEFT: Arsenal fans standing outside their houses in Fife Street, Islington, are caught up in FA Cup Final fever on 5 May 1972. Despite the fans' best efforts, Leeds United won 1–0.

ABOVE: Young fans read the poster announcing the postponement of the Arsenal v Preston match due to fog, 6 December 1952.

RIGHT: Supporters gather at the main entrance at Highbury waiting to collect autographs of the team after training, 14 August 1946.

ABOVE: Young fans in the queue to watch Arsenal play Tottenham at Highbury in the third round of the FA Cup, 8 January 1949. Arsenal won 3-0.

RIGHT: Fans queue up hours before the first-ever north London derby in the FA Cup, 8 January 1949.

ABOVE: Boring Arsenal! An Arsenal fan yawns during a friendly with Glasgow Rangers at Highbury, 17 October 1951.

LEFT: With Highbury sold out, some Arsenal fans find novel ways to watch the match with Burnley, 14 February 1948. Arsenal won 3-0.

RIGHT: Arsenal supporters queue to enter Arsenal tube station in October 1951 after Arsenal hosted Glasgow Rangers.

ABOVE: Arsenal captain Tom Parker and Huddersfield captain Tommy Parker lead out their teams before the 1930 FA Cup Final. This was the first time the captains walked onto the pitch side-by-side as a mark of respect for the Arsenal manager and former Huddersfield manager, Herbert Chapman. Chapman's Arsenal won the final 2-0.

ABOVE: King George V meets the team before the FA Cup Final at Wembley, 26 April 1930. It was the day in which, right on cue, his five-year plan for Arsenal bore fruit with the Club's first trophy.

ABOVE: The recording of the 1998 FA Cup Final song was an exuberant affair with Ian Wright, Christopher Wreh and Luis Boa Morte leading the chorus.

RIGHT: The Arsenal squad record their FA Cup Final song at Columbia Studios, 30 March 1932. The other side of the record was the recording of their opponents, Newcastle United.

ABOVE: Arsenal captain Joe Mercer makes the introductions as Prime Minister Winston Churchill shakes hands with the team prior to the brave FA Cup Final defeat to Newcastle United, 3 May 1952. Arsenal finished the game with only eight fit men. Mercer said: 'I thought the greatest honour was to play for my country. I was wrong. It was to captain Arsenal today'. Arsenal lost the match 1-0.

RIGHT: Goalmouth action from the 1936 FA Cup Final against Sheffield United at Wembley. Arsenal won 1-0 to crown the Club's fiftieth anniversary. In a game requiring grit and determination, Ted Drake drove home the winner from the edge of the area, 25 April 1936.

ABOVE: Arsenal celebrate with a lap of honour following the 2-1 League Cup Final victory over Liverpool, 5 April 1987.

ABOVE: Tony Adams lifts the FA Cup following a 2-0 victory over Newcastle United which secured the Club's second Double, 16 May 1998.

LEFT: Tom Parker parades the FA Cup, the Club's first major honour, in 1930. It was to herald a period of domination. Throughout the 1930s spectators watched spellbound as the Gunners switched from defence to attack with thrilling and devastating efficiency. The team put on an exhilarating spectacle for an audience badly in need of escape from the misery of economic depression and imminent war.

LEFT: The Arsenal team visit Wembley prior to the 1971 FA Cup Final.

FOLLOWING PAGES: 'It's not every day a north London lad, a bit of scruff from one of the local estates, hits the goal that not only wins the FA Cup but clinches the first Double in the history of their own club. It's the stuff of dreams', said Charlie George. Arsenal faced Liverpool on a hot, energy-sapping afternoon in the 1971 FA Cup Final. Both teams were wilting when, late in extra time, the King of Highbury unleashed a screamer into the net before sinking to his knees in sheer joy and exhaustion. Arsenal won the game 2-1.

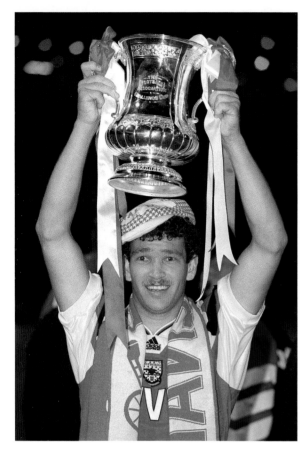

ABOVE: John Jensen celebrates with the FA Cup after Andy Linighan's goal in the final seconds of extra time completed a 2-1 replay victory over Sheffield Wednesday, 20 May 1993. It also clinched a unique FA Cup and League Cup Double – the first time a Cup Double was achieved. Wednesday had been defeated in both finals.

RIGHT: Frank McLintock collects the FA Cup from the Duke of Kent after a 2-1 victory over Liverpool at Wembley, 8 May 1971. It put an end to talk of his Wembley curse, after McLintock had lost five previous finals - two with Arsenal and three with Leicester City.

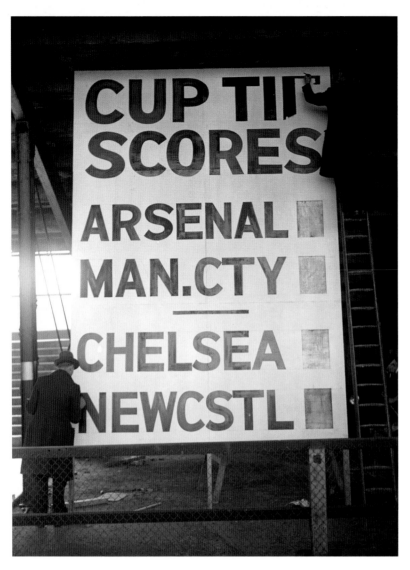

ABOVE: A scoreboard at the White City stadium in London enables spectators at an Oxford and Cambridge University sports event to keep in touch with Arsenal's FA Cup semi-final against Manchester City at Villa Park, March 1932. Arsenal won 1-0.

RIGHT: Following a 1-0 victory over Sheffield United Alex James carries the FA Cup around Wembley with Eddie Hapgood carrying the plinth. Joe Hulme looks on with George Allison, 25 April 1936.

ABOVE: Steve Morrow's League Cup Final celebrations are curtailed as captain Tony Adams drops him shortly after the final whistle, breaking the midfielder's arm, 18 April 1993. Arsenal beat Sheffield Wednesday 2–1 at Wembley.

ABOVE: Goal scorer Paul Merson with the League Cup and Man of the Match award, 18 April 1993. Merson put in an inspirational performance including scoring a twentieth minute equalizer.

ABOVE: Club captain Joe Mercer carries the FA Cup after Arsenal had beaten Liverpool 2-0 at Wembley on 29 April 1950. Reg Lewis' brace had secured the trophy for a side with an average age of over 30, still the oldest ever FA Cup winners.

RIGHT: Joe Mercer holds aloft the FA Cup on 29 April 1950. Liverpool-based Mercer, who had trained with Arsenal's opponents in the weeks leading up to the match, was presented with a loser's medal before the error was spotted.

ABOVE: Arsenal captain Frank McLintock talks to a young supporter as he sits with the FA Cup on the steps of Islington Town Hall. The Arsenal team had gathered there to celebrate the 1971 League and Cup Double.

LEFT: The Arsenal team celebrate their 3–2 win over Manchester United in the FA Cup Final in 1979. Front row (left to right) Liam Brady, Pat Rice, Sammy Nelson, Brian Talbot. Back row (left to right) Steve Walford, David Price, Pat Jennings, Willie Young, Alan Sunderland, David O'Leary, Frank Stapleton, Graham Rix.

RIGHT: Thousands of fans descend on Islington Town Hall to welcome back the victorious team after their first FA Cup win, beating Huddersfield 2-0 at Wembley, 29 April 1930.

FOLLOWING PAGES: Patrick Vieira strikes the ball for the last time as an Arsenal player in a competitive fixture, clinching the 2005 FA Cup in a 5-4 penalty shoot-out victory over Manchester United, 21 May 2005.